Jesus Comes to Me

Preparation for First Confession
and First Holy Communion

by Dora Nash

© ST PAULS 2010

Revised edition 2015

Reprint 2016, 2017, 2019

ISBN 978-0-85439-920-8

Set in Sassoon Primary

Pictures courtesy of Our Lady's Catechists,
Enid Chadwick, and the author.

Nihil Obstat: The Rev. Paul Dean STB, MA
Censor of Books
Imprimatur: +Vincent Nichols
Archbishop of Birmingham
Birmingham, 13 February 2008

ST PAULS Publishing
ST PAULS by Westminster Cathedral
Morpeth Terrace, Victoria
London, SW1P 1EP
Tel: +44 (0) 207 828 5582
www.stpauls.org.uk

ST PAULS Publishing Ireland
Moyglare Road
Maynooth
Co. Kildare, Ireland
Tel: +353 (0)1 6285 933
www.stpauls.ie

ST PAULS is an activity of the priests and brothers
of the Society of St Paul who proclaim the Gospel
through the media of social communication.

Printed in Malta by Melita Press.

Contents

To my family

Dear parents, priests, catechists and teachers,

This course is to help you prepare your children for First Confession and First Communion. It is divided into eighteen chapters. Each chapter follows a similar pattern. First there is a black and white picture to colour alongside a page of text. There are two levels of text: that in smaller type at the foot of the page is more advanced and could be omitted depending on the ability of the participants. The font used throughout is a recommended Sassoon font designed for the early years of reading.

The second page of each chapter provides a variety of activities: simple writing tasks, puzzles, drawing and learning, with suggestions for extension activities in the **More to do** section. The learning section mainly focuses on prayers which every Catholic child should know and the other activities either reinforce the material presented in the text or give an opportunity for input from the child in terms of drawing, reading or expressive writing. At the end of each chapter there are some catechism-style questions for you to use where appropriate and in any way that you wish. Half way through and at the end there are quizzes which will help you to assess the quality of learning. The material could be used more flexibly if you wish. For example, the chapters specific to First Confession – 6,7,8, and 9 – could be used later in the sequence if it suits your own requirements.

The adult overseeing the delivery of the programme will need to do some minimal preparation prior to each session. Some activities will need ordinary or coloured pencils, and others will need extra paper or scissors. You may need to provide envelopes for keeping tidy the cut-out features. In some cases a simple Scripture passage, or a picture, may need to be prepared. The extension activities, if you decide to use them, might involve a visit to the church, a task to be done at home or some information to be found.

I hope that you and the children find this course formative and fun and that their First Confession and First Communion days will be memorable milestones in their life-long love of Our Lord Jesus Christ and his Church.

Dora Nash

1. God Made Everything

God saw all that he had made
and it was very good

In the beginning there was God. He made the whole world and everything in it. He made it all out of nothing.

He made the sun and moon, the planets, and all living things on the earth. He made fish, birds and animals. And he made human beings. He loved all that he made, but human beings were special.

God made human beings so that they could think, make things and plan. He also made them so they could love each other and him. He wanted them to get to know him as their Father and talk to him.

He gave them the beautiful world to live in.

You can read all about the story of Creation in the first part of the Bible: the Book of Genesis. The Bible writer called the first man and woman Adam and Eve and wrote that they were more than animals – they were made 'in the image and likeness of God'. This means that while the human body is a physical thing, we also have **souls**, each made specially by God. Our soul makes us be like God because it makes us able to learn and invent, to think, decide and choose. Because we are like God, we can know him and love him. He is our Creator and our Father and he wants us to be with him in happiness for ever.

To do

Here is the word CREATION, written down the page. Write on the dotted lines the name of something God made which begins with each of the letters:

c *at*

r *at*

e *lephants*

a *nt's*

t *rees*

i *nsects*

o *ctopuse*

n *ote*

Make up your own prayer, praising God for the wonderful things he has made, using the letters of a word to start each line (this is called an acrostic). You could use BEAUTIFUL or WORLD, or choose one of your own.

To learn

Glory be to the Father, and to the Son, and to the Holy Spirit. As it was in the beginning, is now and ever shall be, world without end. Amen.

To write

Put the right word from the list in each gap:

God made everything out of ... *nothing* ...

He made human beings to be like ... *him* ...

God wanted humans to ... *love* ... him and each other.

We are like God because we have ... *Sols* ...

God is our ... *father* ... and our ... *Creator* ...

Creator   him   love   Father   souls   nothing

More things to do

Find a Bible and look at the first chapter of Genesis – the story of the Creation.

A famous artist long ago – Michelangelo – painted a beautiful picture of God creating on the ceiling of a famous Chapel in Rome. See if you can find a copy at home or on the internet.

Make a list of all the things that humans can do which show we are made 'in the image of God'.

Make a prayer book of your own so that you can copy into it all the prayers in this book. Make an attractive cover for it. Copy in the Glory Be.

QUESTION: Who made you?   ANSWER: God made me.

QUESTION: Why did God make you?   ANSWER: God made me to know him, love him and serve him in this world and to be happy with him for ever in the next.

2. We Need God to Save Us

Moses is given the Ten Commandments

God made us free to choose to be good or to be bad. We can love each other or be selfish. We can **worship** God or we can disobey him.

At the very beginning, human beings wanted their own way. They did not want to do what God knew was right for them. They thought they knew better than God did. They chose to do wrong and lost God's friendship. Because of their bad choice, humans now had to suffer death instead of being with God for ever.

Ever since then, all human beings have behaved selfishly. This is called **Original Sin**. We are all tempted to do wrong things or think wrong thoughts. We must try not to act or think wrongly. These bad actions and thoughts keep us from God and make us unhappy. Actions and thoughts which keep us from God are called **sins**. But God still loves us always because we are his children. He helps and rescues us. He teaches us right and wrong. He forgives us when we sin.

Because humans were selfish and sinned, God has had to teach us what is right all over again. He first spoke to **Abraham** who had a great love for God and who did obey him. In return God made him the father of a new nation – Israel. God rescued the people of Israel when they were made into slaves in Egypt and he gave them wonderful food in the desert when they were hungry. He gave some laws to their leader **Moses** so that the people of Israel would know what was right and wrong. The laws that he gave to Moses are called the **Ten Commandments**. God then gave them their own country to live in and sent them kings and other leaders called **prophets** to help them keep his laws. He wanted them to become his friends again.

To learn

The Ten Commandments:

1. I am the Lord your God: you must not worship anything else.

2. Do not use God's name to swear.

3. Keep Sunday holy for worshipping God.

4. Honour your father and mother.

5. Do not kill.

6. Do not take someone else's wife or husband.

7. Do not steal.

8. Do not tell lies about someone.

9. Do not long for someone else's wife or husband.

10. Do not long for anything that belongs to someone else.

To do

Match the words on the left with the scrambled words on the right:

ABRAHAM	**AVDDI**
MOSES	**LDAIEN**
SAMUEL	**OOONMSL**
DAVID	**ASAIHI**
SOLOMON	**HABAMRA**
ISAIAH	**LUSAEM**
DANIEL	**SSOEM**

More things to do

Find out about some of the people whose names are jumbled up. See if you can read about them in a children's Bible.

Draw your own stone tablets for the Ten Commandments and write them on in the correct order.

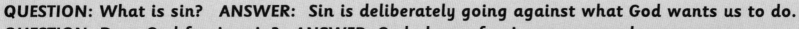

? **QUESTION: What is sin?   ANSWER: Sin is deliberately going against what God wants us to do.
QUESTION: Does God forgive sin?   ANSWER: God always forgives anyone who says sorry.
QUESTION: Can we save ourselves from sin on our own?   ANSWER: We need God to save us with his love and his help.**

3. Jesus is God's Son

Holy Mary Mother of God

For many years God sent leaders and prophets to the people of Israel to help them to love and obey him. But God wanted to speak to all his people in a way that was even better. He wanted to send his own Son.

His Son would teach us, help us and rescue us from sin and death for ever.

God chose the right time and place for his Son to be born as a man. He chose a young woman to be his mother, and he kept her specially free from sin. Her name was **Mary**. She gave birth to God's son.

God told her to call him **Jesus**. This means 'Saviour'. Jesus is God and also Man. He is God's only Son, and also human like us, except that he never sinned. Only he can bring us back to friendship with God his Father. He is God the Father's greatest gift to us.

Jesus is both God and Man – we say that he is divine and human. This is called the **Incarnation**: God has become a man. This was the way that God chose to bring us back to him. Jesus came to show us how to love God and to take away sin for ever. God needed someone to help him to do this. God asked Mary to be the mother of his Son. An angel, Gabriel, brought her the message and she agreed to it, even though she did not completely understand it herself. She showed great faith in God. We honour her and pray to her. She is our Mother too. We also call her Our Lady.

To write

Put the right word from the list in each gap:

Jesus is both God and ....*man*........... .

Jesus's mother is ...*Mary*...... .

She was free from ....*sin*..... .

Jesus's father is ....*god*......... .

Jesus was born at the first ...*christmas*...... .

Jesus was born to .....*save*..... us.

God   man   Christmas   save   Mary   sin

To learn

Hail Mary, full of grace, the Lord is with thee.
Blessed art thou among women
and blessed is the fruit of thy womb, Jesus.
Holy Mary, Mother of God,
pray for us sinners
now and at the hour of our death.
Amen.

To draw

You will already know the Christmas story.
Draw your favourite part of the story in this space.

More to do

Think of a carol that you sing at Christmas. Can you remember what it says about Jesus?

Find a map of the Holy Land and look for Bethlehem, Nazareth and Jerusalem on it. These are the special places in Jesus's life. Do you know why?

Look in your church to find a statue of Our Lady – what is she doing? What is she wearing?

Find out about the Rosary and how to pray it. You could draw some rosary beads and label the drawing, and learn the mysteries of the Rosary. There are twenty altogether.

?   **QUESTION: Who is Jesus?   ANSWER:** *Jesus is God's only Son who was born a man to save us.*
QUESTION: Who is Mary?   ANSWER: *Mary is the Mother of God, chosen to give birth to God the Son, Jesus.*

4. Being Baptised

For thirty years Jesus lived quietly with Mary his mother and Joseph her husband in Nazareth. Then Jesus knew that the time had come for him to start his work. His work was to tell the people about how much God loved them. He had to tell them to be sorry for their sins.

Jesus went to a river called the River Jordan. His cousin, John, was teaching the people there that God was going to send someone wonderful to show them the way to be holy. John knew that Jesus was that wonderful person. He knew Jesus was God's Son.

Jesus was baptised by John in the river. This was to show that he was starting his work. The people heard God the Father's voice and saw the Holy Spirit. They knew then that Jesus had come from God.

We are baptised when we are very small. Our parents want us to become friends and followers of Jesus. Baptism cleans us of Original Sin and makes us God's own children.

When we are baptised we become part of the Catholic **Church**. God's Holy Spirit comes down on us like he did at Jesus's baptism. The holy water is poured over our heads as the priest says:

'I baptise you in the name of the Father and of the Son and of the Holy Spirit.' From that moment we are Christians – part of God's family. The water shows that God is cleaning us from sin and giving us his loving help to make us grow, like a plant being watered. This 'loving help' is called **grace**.

We are able to have all our sins forgiven and washed away by God because Jesus died on the cross. He gave himself up for us so that we could become friends with God again. He died for our sins.

To write

Put the right word from the list in each gap:

Jesus was ....*baptised*.... in the River

Jordan. When we are baptised we become part of

God's ....*the ~~party~~*....
water
....~~family~~.... is used in baptism to show

that God is ....*washing ~~the~~*.... away our sin.

Plants will ....*die*.... if they are not watered,

and we need the water of ....*baptism*.... to

give our souls new....*life*....

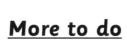

washing   life   baptised   die
baptism   family   water

To do

Join the dots to find a big basin used for baptism, called a font.

Find out what happens at a Baptism. You could act the occasion out with friends, with everyone taking different roles. You could use a doll for the baby.

More to do

At home, find a picture of your baptism.

What colour does the baby wear? Why?

Ask your parents where you were baptised and on what date.

Find out who your God-parents are.

See if you still have your candle which was given to you at your baptism – what does it have on it?

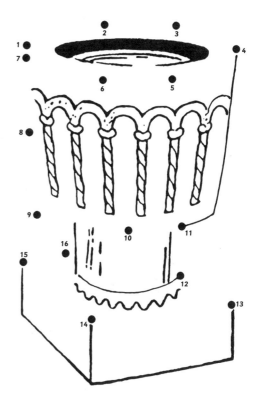

? QUESTION: What is baptism? ANSWER: Baptism is an action by God in which he washes away Original Sin, gives us new life and makes us his children. It is the first Sacrament.
QUESTION: What are the other Sacraments? ANSWER: There are seven Sacraments: baptism, confession (or penance), holy communion, confirmation, marriage, ordination, and the anointing of the sick.

5. Jesus Calls People to Follow Him

'Go and make disciples of all nations, baptising them and teaching them.'

When he had been baptised, Jesus began to travel about the land teaching the people about God's love. Many of the people who listened to Jesus became his good friends. We call them the **disciples**. By our baptism we are Jesus's disciples too. We believe in him and love him and want to do what he says.

The first four disciples were called Peter, Andrew, James and John. These four and eight others were chosen by Jesus to be his special helpers called **the twelve apostles.** They travelled with him and helped him to teach others. He sent them out to take his message to all the world.

Later, the apostles carried on Jesus's work when he went away. They taught and preached, they baptised people and forgave sins. They made sick people better and said Mass. They were the first priests and bishops. The Catholic Church goes back to the apostles and carries on Jesus's work today. We are proud to be members of Jesus's Church.

Jesus's followers today are called the Church. In the Catholic Church there are bishops, priests, deacons and people. The Church is the People of God. We are all baptised and carry on Jesus's work. We all have a duty to follow Jesus's teaching. We know about his teaching through the Gospels and through what the Church tells us.

Priests do Jesus's work in a special way, like the twelve apostles did. Only they can forgive sins in **Confession** and say Mass. Some priests have the work of ruling and guiding the Church: we call them **bishops**. The most important bishop is the Pope. He is Bishop of Rome and the head of the whole Catholic Church. St Peter was the first Pope.

To learn

The disciples asked Jesus how to pray. He told them this prayer:

Our Father who art in heaven
Hallowed be thy name.
Thy kingdom come.
Thy will be done on earth as it is
in heaven.
Give us this day our daily bread
and forgive us our trespasses
as we forgive those who
trespass against us.
And lead us not into temptation
but deliver us from evil.
Amen.

To do

A crossword about the Church. Read the clues and fit the answers in next to the correct number on the crossword square. Some go across and some go down.

Across

1. There were twelve . . .
2. Another word for followers
3. We pray for God's . . . to come

Down

4. A . . . says Mass
5. The Pope is the . . . of Rome
6. The first Pope

More to do

In a children's Bible find a list of the twelve apostles' names and write them out.

Find out the names of your priest and bishop. Where does the bishop live?

QUESTION: What is a disciple? ANSWER: A disciple is someone who is baptised and who follows Jesus.
QUESTION: What is a priest? ANSWER: A priest is a man chosen and ordained to serve God's people.
QUESTION: What is the Church? ANSWER: The Church is God's people.
QUESTION: What does Catholic mean? ANSWER: Catholic means universal – that is, "found everywhere" and "for everybody".

6. Jesus Saves and Heals Us

Jesus gives us life and happiness

Jesus spent a lot of his time with people who were in great need. He loved the sick people and made them well. He talked to sinners and told them that God loved them. He made friends with the poor and the rich alike.

One day an important man came to see Jesus. His name was Jairus. Jairus's little daughter was very ill. He and his wife were worried and asked Jesus to come and see her. They knew that he could make their little girl well. But by the time Jesus got to the house, the little girl had died.

Jesus and the parents went into her room. Jesus took her by the hand and said 'Little girl, I tell you to get up.' And she came back to life straight away. Her parents were full of joy.

Jesus can make us better in every way. He brings us happiness and makes everything right again. He can conquer all evil, even death.

Jairus and his wife had great faith in Jesus. They trusted him to bring health and life to their daughter. Jesus is God so he can do this. He saves us too when we need it and will never turn us away. When we are worried or ill, we should pray to him. When we have sinned, we should ask for his help and **forgiveness**. Our sickness can be in our body or in our soul. Jesus heals us in our body and in our soul too. Catholics receive Jesus's healing and forgiveness in the Sacrament of **Penance** or Confession.

To write

Put the right word from the list in each gap:

Jairus and his wife had a ...*daughter*...

who was very ...*ill*.... . They had great

...*faith*... in Jesus. They asked him to make

her ...*well*... again. Jesus brought her back to

...*life*... after she had died. We turn to Jesus too

when we are ...*worried*... . He can heal us in

body and ...*soul*.... . He heals our soul in

the Sacrament of ...*Penance*........ .

life   **Penance**   **daughter**   **faith**
ill   **worried**   **well**   **soul**

Now write a prayer thanking God for your family and friends and all the good things you have.

To do

From the Bible read another story of Jesus healing someone. Draw a picture of it here:

To learn

We pray for those who have died using this prayer:

Eternal rest grant unto them O Lord
And let perpetual light shine upon them.
May they rest in peace.   Amen.

More to do

Find out about Lourdes – a town in France where sick people go on pilgrimage to pray.

?   QUESTION: What is a sacrament?   ANSWER: A sacrament is an action or some words in which God gives us his grace.
QUESTION: What is grace? ANSWER: Grace is God's loving help which he gives to us freely to save us.

7. Jesus Loves Us All

'If I have robbed anyone I will pay them back four times the amount.'

One day Jesus was walking through a town with his disciples. He saw a man sitting up in a tree. The man's name was Zacchaeus. He wanted to see Jesus. Nobody liked Zacchaeus because he took money from them. His job was to give the money to the government. But he took more than he should, and kept a lot of it for himself. This was stealing.

Jesus knew that the man was sorry for stealing from the people. He said to him 'Zacchaeus! Come down! I want to have tea at your house!' Everyone was very surprised because Zacchaeus was a sinner. They thought that Jesus would not like him.

When they had finished the meal, Zacchaeus said to Jesus: 'I am very sorry for stealing from the people. I want to make everything right again. I will give back to them much more money than I took from them to show how sorry I am.' Jesus was very pleased with him and said that Zacchaeus was saved from his evil ways.

We are like Zacchaeus: we all sin sometimes. We need Jesus to forgive us and save us from our evil ways. We must first know what we have done wrong and then tell Jesus we are sorry. Then we must make up for what we have done. We can do all this when we go to the Sacrament of Penance or Confession.

God is always ready to forgive our sins. No sin is too big to be forgiven by God. Jesus died on the cross to take away our sins: he did nothing wrong but he paid for our sins with his life. Very serious sins are called **mortal sins.** They separate us from God and take away the grace in our souls. We need to go to Confession to be forgiven for mortal sins and to receive his grace so we can start again, and love God more.

To do

Find these words hidden in the puzzle below:

penance   **Zacchaeus**   **tree**   **stealing**

sorry   **evil**   **money**   **saved**

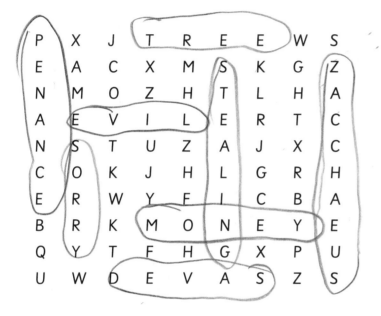

Tick the words off when you have found them.

To do

Read the story of the Lost Son in St Luke's Gospel. Find the words that the son plans to say to his Father. Write them in this speech bubble:

More to do

From the Bible, read the story of the centurion's servant: what message does the centurion send to Jesus? Listen out for words like these in the Mass.

?   **QUESTION:** What is a mortal sin? **ANSWER:** A mortal sin is a serious offence against God. Mortal sins must be confessed in the Sacrament of Penance.

QUESTION: What are less serious sins called? **ANSWER:** Less serious sins are called venial sins. We must still ask for God's forgiveness for venial sins.

8. Getting ready for your First Confession

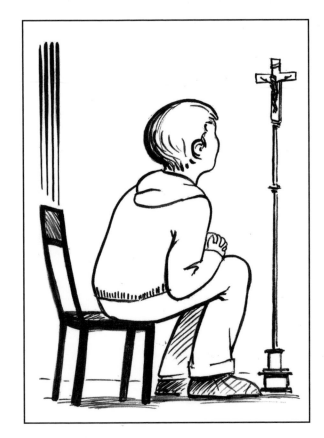

When we pray we raise our hearts and minds to God

You are getting ready to make your First Confession. Confession or Penance is one of the seven sacraments. We say sorry to God for any sins we have done because this spoils our friendship with him. Sin offends God our loving Father. Jesus died to say sorry to God for all our sins. In the Sacrament of Penance God forgives us and fills us with his loving help – his grace.

Jesus gave his apostles the power to forgive sins. Catholic priests do the apostles' work today. When we go to Confession we tell our sins to the priest. This is how we tell Jesus that we are sorry for the wrong things we have done or said or thought.

God has given every human being a way of telling whether we are doing right or wrong. This is called our **conscience**. Everyone should listen to their conscience – it is God's voice in us. We should obey what our conscience tells us, because it is God telling us. When we were very little, we did not know about right and wrong. Now we are old enough to hear our conscience and we can think about what we have done or what we are going to do.

Even without being taught, we can all know the difference between right and wrong. Our conscience tells us. We must listen carefully to our parents, priests and teachers too, so that we know that we are hearing our conscience correctly.

We should all examine our conscience every night before we go to sleep as part of our night prayers and ask God to forgive any wrong thing we have done during the day. This will also help us to remember what sins we need to confess when we go to receive the Sacrament of Penance next time.

To know

Copy this out onto some coloured card and use it when you are thinking about what to say in Confession:

Examination of Conscience

Have I been unkind to anyone?

Have I told any lies?

Have I broken any promises?

Have I taken something which is not mine?

Have I been disobedient?

Have I said any bad words?

Have I been greedy or jealous?

Have I been lazy or careless?

Have I been angry or rude?

Have I failed to do something good?

Have I deliberately hurt anybody?

Have I always put myself first?

Have I deliberately missed saying my prayers?

Have I deliberately missed going to Mass?

Have I offended God in any other way?

To learn

You will need to know this prayer for your First Confession:

Act of Contrition

O my God
because you are so good
I am very sorry that I have sinned against you
and by the help of your grace
I will not sin again.

More to do

Find the Confessional in your church or ask where Confession takes place. What does it look like? Where will you kneel or sit? Where will the priest be?

Write a story about a boy or girl who does something wrong and then is sorry and asks forgiveness.

Read the story in the Bible about the paralysed man whom Jesus cured. What were Jesus's first words to the man?

. . . .

. . . .

Make sure you have copied all the prayers so far into your prayer book.

? QUESTION: **What does the Sacrament of Penance do?** ANSWER: *The Sacrament of Penance gives us God's forgiveness for our sins and fills us with his grace to help us not to sin again.*
QUESTION: **Who hears confessions?** ANSWER: *The priest hears confessions and forgives us in God's name on behalf of the Church.*

9. Making your First Confession

'Your sins are forgiven.'

Your parents, teacher or priest will let you know when you will make your First Confession and where to go to. This is about what to do. Before you go in, you must think quietly about what sins you have done. Use the questions from the last chapter to help you. Try hard to remember them all. You must say them all to the priest, leaving nothing out.

There are four parts to the Sacrament of Penance:

1. we tell the priest what sins we have done
2. we say sorry for our sins
3. we make up for what we have done
4. the priest gives us God's forgiveness and grace.

First of all, say 'Bless me Father. This is my First Confession. Here are my sins.' Tell him all the sins you thought of when you examined your conscience. The priest will talk to you for a little while about how you can try not to sin again. Then he will give you God's forgiveness. You must say the 'Act of Contrition' from the last chapter. The priest will give you a little act of penance to do – a prayer perhaps. Then go out quietly and kneel down in the church to say your penance prayers.

God forgives you of all the sins you confess to the priest if you are truly sorry for them and promise to try not to sin again. God's loving help, or grace, which comes from God to you in this sacrament will help you do this.

To write

These are the names for the four parts of the Sacrament of Penance or Confession.

Copy out the words from the page opposite which explain the words:

1. Confession – we tell ..... _Peranc_ .....

2. Contrition – we say ..... _Bless you_ .....

3. Penance – we make up ..... _Sns_ .....

4. Absolution – the priest ..... _Confesson_ .....

To do

Match the words on the left with the scrambled words on the right:

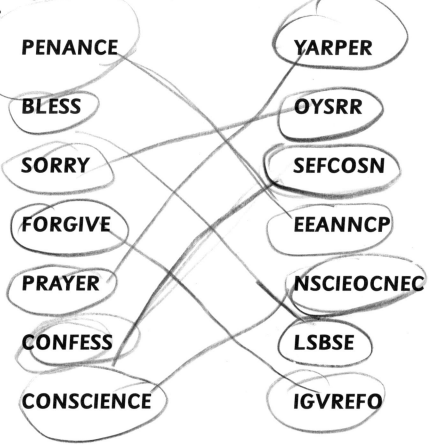

PENANCE   YARPER

BLESS   OYSRR

SORRY   SEFCOSN

FORGIVE   EEANNCP

PRAYER   NSCIEOCNEC

CONFESS   LSBSE

CONSCIENCE   IGVREFO

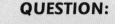

QUESTION: What are the four parts of the Sacrament of Penance? **ANSWER:** The four parts of the Sacrament of Penance are Confession, Contrition, Penance and Absolution.

QUESTION: Why must I do penance? **ANSWER:** Penance makes up for the wrong done.

What have you learned so far? Test yourself

1. Who were the first four disciples of Jesus?
2. How many sacraments are there?
3. What is the name of the man who climbed a tree to see Jesus?
4. Who baptised Jesus in the River Jordan?
5. What is the name of Jesus's mother?
6. How many apostles did Jesus choose?
7. What is the fourth commandment?
8. What did Jesus say to Jairus's daughter?
9. Which is the first sacrament we receive?
10. Name two prophets from the Old Testament.
11. Which apostle of Jesus was the first Pope?
12. Who was given the Ten Commandments by God?
13. What does the word 'Catholic' mean?
14. What is another name for the Sacrament of Penance?
15. What are the four parts of the Sacrament of Penance?

More difficult questions – try them:

16. What is the soul?
17. What is Original Sin?
18. What is grace?
19. What does the Incarnation mean?
20. What do we call very serious sins against God?

See the answers on page 25.

Answers

1. Peter, Andrew, James and John
2. Seven
3. Zacchaeus
4. John the Baptist – Jesus's cousin
5. Mary
6. Twelve
7. Honour your father and mother
8. 'Little girl, get up.'
9. Baptism
10. Samuel, Isaiah or Daniel
11. Peter
12. Moses
13. 'Found everywhere' and 'for everyone'
14. The Sacrament of Confession or Reconciliation
15. Contrition, Confession, Absolution and Penance

16. The soul is the part of us which is not our body, and which makes us like God
17. Original Sin is the sinfulness we all have because the first humans rejected God
18. Grace is God's loving help which he gives to us when we are baptised
19. God becoming a human being – Jesus
20. Mortal sins

How many right answers did you get?

10. Jesus does wonderful things

'Do whatever Jesus tells you' said Mary

Jesus and his mother Mary were invited to a wedding. They travelled to Cana which was near Nazareth where they lived. They ate and drank at the wedding feast with the other guests. After a while they noticed that the people serving the meal looked worried. 'We have run out of wine' they said.

Mary looked at Jesus. She knew that he had God's power because he was God's Son. She knew that he could do wonderful things. She told the servants to do whatever Jesus said.

Jesus said to the servants, 'Fill those big jars up to the top with water.' They filled up six huge jars to the brim. Jesus said to them 'Now pour some out and give it to the man in charge to taste.' The man said 'This is the best wine I have ever tasted!' The servants knew that Jesus had worked a miracle: he had turned the water into wine.

We drink wine on a special occasion, to celebrate something with our friends and family. Wine can also be used to heal and make things clean. Jesus wants to give us healing and happiness always. At Mass, through the power of God, the wine is changed into Jesus's Blood so that we can be very close to him, and be filled with joy.

Jesus drank wine at the Last Supper with his disciples and said that it was his Blood, given for them to drink. This is why we use wine in the Mass. God does something wonderful with the wine just as Jesus turned the water into wine with a miracle. The wine becomes the Blood of Jesus, giving us joy and health and joining us to Jesus in the great feast of the Mass. Jesus told his disciples that he was like a Vine and they were its branches: we must not cut ourselves off from him or we will wither.

Crucifix	Crucifix	Altar	Tabernacle	Tabernacle	Crucifix
Tabernacle	Tabernacle	Chalice	Tabernacle	Host	Crucifix
Host	Host	Altar	Host	Altar	Crucifix
Altar	Altar	Chalice	Host	Chalice	Crucifix
Chalice	Chalice	Chalice	Altar	Host	Tabernacle

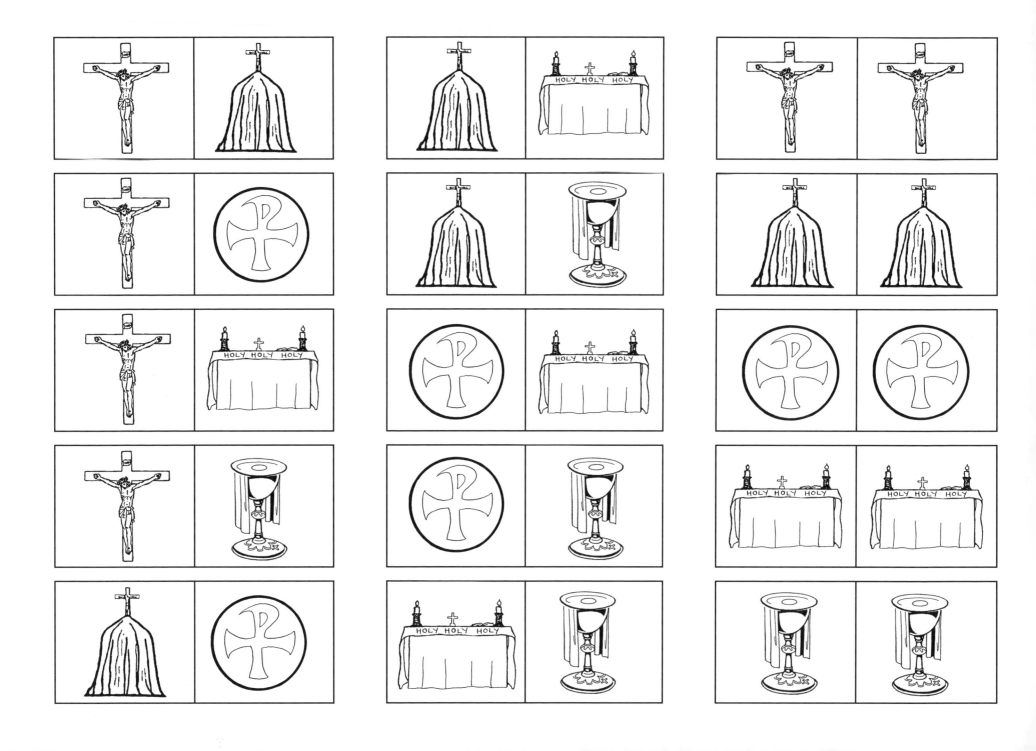

To write

Imagine that you are one of the guests at the wedding at Cana. Write the story of what happened in your own words.

To do

Which of the lines leads into the jar?

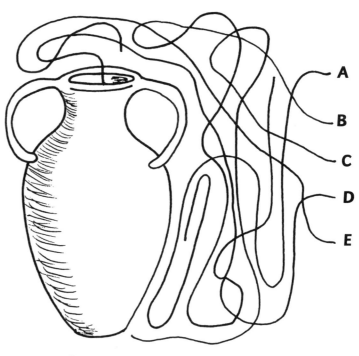

A

B

C

D

E

More to do

Look out at Mass for the Offertory Procession when the wine is taken up to the altar. What else is taken with it? What does the priest do with it? Listen out for wine being mentioned in the Mass.

Find out at home in a book or on the internet about how wine is made. What is it made from?

To learn

Lord Jesus I love you
Lord Jesus I praise you
Lord Jesus I thank you
Lord Jesus I shall follow you every day of my life

?

QUESTION: **What is a miracle?** **ANSWER:** **A miracle is a wonderful thing which God does which has no other explanation.**

QUESTION: **What is wine used for in the Mass?** **ANSWER:** **In Mass, God turns the wine into Jesus's blood for us to receive at Communion.**

11. Jesus feeds the hungry

People loved to listen to Jesus teaching them about God. They came from miles around to hear him. One day, Jesus went out into the hills and a great crowd followed him there to listen to him. There were more than 5000 people there. They stayed all day.

In the evening, the disciples told Jesus that the people were hungry. There was nowhere to buy anything. It was too late to go home. Jesus felt very sorry for them all and wanted to help them. He said 'Is there no food at all?' The disciples found a boy who had five small loaves of bread and two fish. The boy gave the food to Jesus.

Jesus looked up to heaven and blessed the bread and fish. Then he broke it into pieces and gave it to the disciples. The disciples shared it out among the huge crowd. There was plenty for everyone, and lots left over. Jesus had fed 5000 people with five loaves and two fish. This was a great miracle. It shows us that Jesus is God, and that he can take away our hunger and fill us up with good and satisfying food. Jesus does this for our souls. Our souls need Jesus to live. Our souls receive Jesus in **Communion**.

There was plenty for everyone and some left over

The Feeding of the 5000 is one of Jesus's greatest miracles. The disciples knew that Jesus had done something amazing. But this miracle has a deep meaning too: Jesus came to bring the love of God to us all. He wants to give us everything we need, both things for the body and things for the soul. Just as bread keeps our bodies strong and healthy, so Jesus feeds our soul. He does this in Holy Communion. The priest takes the bread, blesses it and breaks it, just as Jesus did with the loaves. It becomes Jesus's Body. We receive Jesus in Communion.

To write

Choose the right word from the list and put one in each of the gaps:

A great .... came to hear Jesus teach.

They stayed until it was very .... and they got

.... A boy had ....

loaves and .... fish which he gave to Jesus.

Jesus .... the food and it fed five

.... people.

two   **late**   **crowd**   **thousand**

     five   **hungry**   **blessed**

To learn

This is a prayer to say before meals to thank God
for feeding our bodies and souls:

Bless us, O Lord
and these your gifts
which we are about to receive
from your bounty.
Through Christ Our Lord.   Amen.

To do

Colour in the shapes with dots in to see what the picture is:

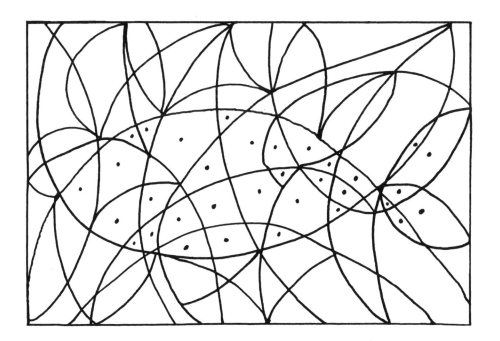

More to do

In the Bible, find and read the story of Jesus cooking fish for
the disciples on the beach (the Gospel of St John chapter 21).

Write a story about the boy who gave the loaves and fish to
Jesus.

 QUESTION: How does Jesus feed us?   ANSWER: He gives us his Body and Blood in the Mass.
QUESTION: What is the bread used for in the Mass?   ANSWER: In Mass, God turns the bread into the
Body of Jesus which we receive at Communion.

12. Jesus is the Bread of Life

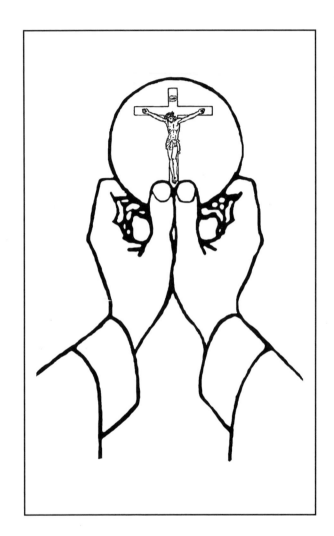

Jesus spoke to the crowd who had just eaten the bread and fish. He said to them 'I am the Bread of Life.' He meant that ordinary bread only filled up their bodies for a little while. He said that he could take away all the longings and emptiness in their souls for ever.

The crowd did not understand Jesus. They wondered how he could feed them for ever. He said to them: 'I am the Bread of Life. Anyone who eats me will live for ever.' The people were very shocked: 'How can we eat a man?' But Jesus told them that his Body was real food and his Blood was real drink for them. If they ate and drank him, they would live for ever. The bread he would give them was his own flesh – given for the life of the world. Some people did not like all this and went away. They did not believe in Jesus. Jesus explained what he meant to those who stayed behind to listen.

The bread that he was talking about is the **Eucharist** – Holy Communion. When Jesus died on the cross, he rescued the whole world from sin, evil and death. And anyone who wanted to be part of this had to receive Jesus at Mass. This was the Bread which saves us for ever: Jesus's Body and Blood in Communion.

In the Old Testament God gave some bread-like food called Manna to the Israelites in the desert, but this had not satisfied their hunger for long. It helped them on their journey and kept them alive. Jesus said that if anyone received the Eucharist, his Body and Blood, then this would be bread of a different kind: the Bread of Life which would make them live for ever in **heaven**.

To do

Find these words in the wordsearch. Tick them off when you have found them:

manna **bread** **Eucharist** **rescued**
Mass **Communion**

W	H	E	U	C	H	A	R	I	S	T
H	O	Q	J	O	L	E	S	S	A	M
B	Y	W	F	M	L	S	P	Z	X	R
R	A	M	C	M	T	B	F	V	A	E
E	Q	W	A	U	N	W	U	L	K	S
A	R	E	L	N	M	A	N	N	A	C
D	Z	X	H	I	S	L	J	H	I	U
D	E	K	C	O	E	R	D	U	C	E
C	B	N	D	N	U	F	S	W	R	D

To learn

Act of Faith

O my God
I believe in you
and all your Church teaches
because you have said it
and your word is true.

To do

Find five differences between these two pictures:

More to do

Find out how bread is made: what goes into it?

In a Bible, read the story of the manna in the desert.

In a book of saints or on the internet find out about the story of Saint Tarcisius.

? QUESTION: **What is Holy Communion?** ANSWER: **Holy Communion is the way in which Jesus feeds us with his own self to make us holy.**
QUESTION: **What is heaven?** ANSWER: **Heaven is living in happiness forever with God.**

13. Jesus at the Last Supper

'Do this in memory of me.'

Jesus travelled to Jerusalem with his disciples. They were going to take part in a great festival called the **Passover**. This was when the people of Israel remembered how God had saved them when they were slaves in Egypt. They went to the **Temple** to pray and they had a special feast – the Passover supper. At the meal, they all ate lamb and herbs and also bread made without yeast. This made the bread flat. It is called Unleavened Bread. Jesus and his disciples ate it with cups of wine.

When the supper was over, Jesus did something new with the bread and wine which was not part of the old Passover meal. He took the bread and blessed it, then he broke it and gave it to the disciples. He said 'Take this and eat it, for this is my Body which will be given up for you.' He blessed the wine too and passed the cup to them. He said 'Take this and drink it, for this is my Blood which will be poured out for you.' This was the first **Mass**.

Jesus was telling his disciples that he would be arrested and put to death the very next day to take all the sins of the world away. He was going to pay for our sins with his life, but he would rise again. By receiving his Body and Blood in Holy Communion, we remember his saving death and share in his victory over sin.

The Passover was the greatest Jewish feast of the year. Many years before, Moses had led the Israelites out of slavery into freedom. They started a new life. Now, by dying on the cross, Jesus led us out of the sinful ways which kept us far from God. His death brought us back to God's friendship. At the Last Supper, Jesus started the Eucharist. The words he said over the bread and wine are the words said at every Mass by the priest: the words of **Consecration**.

To write

Choose the right word to put into each one of the gaps:

The Jewish people had a great feast called the

.... Jesus celebrated the feast in the city

of .... together with his ....

Jesus took the .... and wine and .... them.

Jesus said that they were his Body and .... He

was going to die the next day to take away the sins of the

....

Blood   **Passover**   **world**   **Jerusalem**

disciples   **bread**   **blessed**

To learn

From the Mass:

Lamb of God, you take away the sins of the world,
have mercy on us.
Lamb of God, you take away the sins of the world,
have mercy on us.
Lamb of God you take away the sins of the world,
grant us peace.

To do

Here is the word 'festival' written down the page. There are 8 other important words on page 32 which start with the letters. The number of spaces will give you a clue. Some letters are done for you:

F _ A S _

E _ Y _ _

S _ P _ _ _

T _ M _ _ _

I _ R _ _ L

V _ _ T _ _ Y

A _ E

L _ _ B

More to do

In the Bible read the story of Jesus washing his disciples' feet at the Last Supper. What did he say he wanted them to learn from it?

Find out about Maundy Thursday – which is the day when we remember the Last Supper. What does Maundy mean?

QUESTION: **What is used in the Mass to become the Body and Blood of Jesus?** **ANSWER:** **Bread and wine become the Body and Blood of Jesus in the Mass**

QUESTION: **What do we call the part of the Mass when this happens?** **ANSWER:** **The bread and wine become the Body and Blood of Jesus at the Consecration.**

14. Jesus dies on the cross for us

'Father forgive them. They do not know what they are doing.'

Soon after the Last Supper was over, Jesus was taken away to prison by the leaders of the people in Jerusalem who did not like him. They said he was a trouble-maker because he did miracles and because many people followed him.

Jesus had never done anything wrong. He is God and was born as a man to teach us about God's love. He wanted everybody to be sorry for their sins and to change their bad ways. Because of this, not everyone liked him. Even one of his apostles, Judas, helped the leaders to arrest Jesus.

Jesus was taken to the Governor who was a Roman. His name was Pontius Pilate. Pontius Pilate did not want trouble-makers. He sent Jesus off to be killed even though he had done no harm. Jesus was nailed to a cross in between two other men who were thieves. After three hours he died.

Jesus wanted to do everything he could to bring us all back to God's friendship. He even allowed himself to be put to death. When he died on the cross, all the sins done by every human being were forgiven by God. As long as we are sorry for what we do wrong, we are forgiven. Jesus's death has put everything right.

Jesus died on a hill called Calvary by being crucified – nailed to a cross. He was innocent. But he accepted death for our sake. It was a **sacrifice** which he gladly made. This was the way in which God wanted to bring us back from sin to eternal life with him. Jesus's act of love has **redeemed** us. It is called the Redemption. We love and worship Jesus for his sacrifice.

To write

In a Bible find the story of Simon of Cyrene. Write about it here, or draw a picture of what Simon did to help Jesus.

To learn

A prayer used during Stations of the Cross:

I love you Jesus, my love above all things.
I repent with my whole heart for having offended you.
Never permit me to separate myself from you again.
Grant that I may love you always
and then do with me what you will.

To do

Find a crucifix in your home, church or school. You will see four letters written at the top of the cross. Put the letters under each other in the space below, and put next to each letter what it stands for.

More to do

In every Catholic church there are some pictures on the walls of Jesus's journey to Calvary. They are called the Stations of the Cross. How many are there? Write a list of what each is called.

 QUESTION: What has Jesus's death done for us? ANSWER: Jesus's death has redeemed us from sin. QUESTION: Why do we say that Jesus's death is a sacrifice? ANSWER: Jesus's death is a sacrifice because he willingly gave up his life for our sake.

15. Jesus rises from the dead

'The Lord is risen indeed.'

Jesus died on the cross on **Good Friday**. His friends buried him in a tomb made of rock in a garden near Jerusalem. Then they went home very sad. On the Sunday morning at dawn one of his disciples, Mary Magdalene, went to the grave. It was empty. She saw a man in the garden. 'Where have they taken the body to?' she asked him. She did not know at first that it was Jesus, alive again. He had risen from the dead. He said to her 'Mary!' Then she knew it was Jesus and fell at his feet full of joy and wonder. This was Easter Sunday.

Jesus also showed himself to his apostles and to many other disciples over the next few weeks. They were all amazed and believed in him. They knew now that he was really God. Only God had the power to rise from the dead. Jesus's death had not been a terrible thing. He had been willing to die on the cross so that he could beat death for ever by rising again.

Forty days after Easter Sunday Jesus went back to his Father in heaven. We believe that one day we will follow Jesus to heaven to be happy with God for ever. We do not need to be afraid of death any more.

We call Jesus's rising from the dead the **Resurrection**. It is one of the most important of all Christian beliefs. Jesus's resurrection proves that all he said was true and that he was the Son of God. It shows that he did save us from sin and death, and that there is life after death. The Resurrection gives the power to the Sacraments so that we are truly washed clean in baptism, really forgiven in Confession and receive the real presence of Jesus in Communion.

To write

Choose the right word to put into each one of the gaps:

On Good Friday Jesus was .... in a tomb. One of his disciples went to visit the tomb on the .... morning. Her name was .... When she got there, the tomb was .... She saw Jesus in the .... but did not realise who he was. He spoke her name and then she knew he had .... from the dead.

Jesus also appeared to many other ....

garden   risen   empty   Sunday

Mary Magdalene   disciples   buried

To learn

This is an Easter prayer to Our Lady:

Queen of heaven rejoice – alleluia!
For he whom you did merit to bear – alleluia!
Has risen as he said – alleluia!
Pray for us to God – alleluia!

To do

Match the words on the left with the scrambled words on the right:

EASTER	**OMTB**
MAGDALENE	**RRRNOICTEESU**
ALLELUIA	**RESTEA**
TOMB	**NEGAMELAD**
REJOICE	**ELLAAIUL**
RESURRECTION	**ICEEJRO**

More to do

Make an Easter garden in a shallow tray with moss for grass, stones for the rocky tomb and a path, and twigs for trees.

In the Bible read the story of the apostle Thomas who would not believe that Jesus had risen. What did he say when he finally saw Jesus alive again?

?   QUESTION: **What do we celebrate at Easter?** ANSWER: **At Easter we celebrate Jesus's resurrection from the dead.**

QUESTION: **In what other way do we celebrate the resurrection?** ANSWER: **We celebrate the Resurrection every Sunday by going to Mass.**

16. We go to Mass

We Catholics show our love for Jesus by going to Mass every Sunday. We show that we believe in him and want to follow him with all his other disciples. At Mass we:

- Listen to his teaching when we hear the Gospel reading.
- Show that we believe all that he taught when we say the Creed.
- Listen again to the words Jesus said at the Last Supper.
- Receive his Body and Blood in Holy Communion.

When we go to Mass, we are at the Last Supper. We are with Jesus on Calvary. God makes Jesus's Death and Resurrection present again on the altar. This is why we call the Mass a Sacrifice.

The Mass is one of the seven Sacraments: bread and wine change into Jesus's Body and Blood so that God can feed our souls. This happens at the Consecration.

The Mass is sometimes called the Eucharist, which means 'thanksgiving'. We thank God for sending his Son to save us and take our sins away. We thank God for feeding us in Communion. The Mass is a holy meal in which God gives us his own life for our food.

Sunday Mass is the time when all Catholics gather together to praise and worship God. We must not miss Mass deliberately – this breaks the third Commandment. It is our weekly public act of **worship**.

The Mass has four main parts: we confess our sins, we listen to God's Word, we offer bread and wine to God and he makes it become Jesus's Body and Blood, and we receive Communion. We must try to learn the prayers and responses of the Mass so that we can play our part.

To write

Fill in the rest of the words by copying them from the opposite page:

At Mass we listen to his teaching ....

....

We also show that we believe ....

....

We listen again to ....

....

At Mass we receive his ....

....

To learn

Holy, holy, holy Lord God of hosts,
Heaven and earth are full of your glory.
Hosanna in the Highest!
Blessed is he who comes in the name of the Lord!
Hosanna in the Highest!

To do

In the middle of this book you will find two sheets of thicker card. One half has a picture of a priest on it.

Colour in the priest, leaving his long garment white. This is called the alb. Cut out the figure carefully.

Cut a slit along the dotted black line near the feet. Cut out the smaller piece too and make a slit in that. Slip the two slits into each other to help the figure to stand up.

On the last page of the book you will find pictures of vestments that the priest wears. The long scarf is called the stole. The top garment is called the chasuble.

Colour and cut them out, being careful not to cut off the tabs.

Fit them on to the priest. You could make copies of the vestments to colour in different colours you see in church.

More to do

At Mass, notice the colour of the priest's clothes and the tabernacle veil. Are they green? Gold? White? Pink? Red? Purple?

Find out what the colours mean.

? QUESTION: What is the Sacrament of the Eucharist? ANSWER: The Eucharist is the Body, Blood, soul and divinity of Jesus Christ under the appearances of bread and wine.
QUESTION: Why do we call the Mass a Sacrifice? ANSWER: The Mass is a Sacrifice because it presents again on the altar the death of Jesus on the cross.

17. Jesus is really present

Jesus is present in the monstrance so we can adore him

In the Mass, the priest uses bread and wine as Jesus did at the Last Supper. He has some **hosts** of bread – these are small, round, flat wafers. He also has a beautiful cup with a stem called a **chalice**. This contains the wine.

At the Consecration, the priest takes a host in his hands and says 'This is my Body'. He takes the chalice and says 'This is the cup of my Blood'. At the consecration the bread and wine change what they really are, though they look the same. Our eyes see the host and the wine still, but our faith tells us that they are now Jesus's Body and Blood.

Jesus is really present on the altar. He is just as much there as he was at the Last Supper and on the cross. We cannot see him in the same way that his friends could, but we believe that he is really with us in the Eucharist. When we receive Holy Communion we are truly eating his Body and drinking his Blood, just as he said we must. We sometimes call this receiving the **Blessed Sacrament**.

Even when Mass is over, Jesus's **Real Presence** does not go away. The priest keeps some hosts in a special box called the **tabernacle**. This is usually behind the altar, raised up so that we can see it. It is covered with a coloured veil. When we go into church we know that we are in Jesus's presence. We adore him. We go down on one knee in an act of worship. This is called **genuflecting**. The red light near the altar tells us if Jesus is there in the tabernacle, really present in the Blessed Sacrament.

Catholics often visit the Blessed Sacrament in church when it is not time for Mass. It is a very good way of praying because Jesus is really there and we can adore him and think about him. Catholics can also receive a blessing with the Eucharist: this is called Benediction. The Eucharist has its own feast day – Corpus Christi, which means Body of Christ. This happens in the summer and some churches hold processions in Jesus's honour.

To do

A crossword about the Church. Read the clues and fit the answers in next to the correct number on the crossword square. Some go across and some go down.

Across

1. The Last _ _ _ _ _ _ _
3. The special box for the hosts
6. A host is a small round _ _ _ _ _
7. Another word for worship
10. Bend the knee
12. The Body and _ _ _ _ _ of Jesus
13. When the bread and wine are changed

Down

2. Jesus is really _ _ _ _ _ _ _ _
4. The priest says Mass at the _ _ _ _ _
5. Cup for the Blood of Christ
8. The Blessed _ _ _ _ _ _ _ _ _
9. This covers the tabernacle
11. 'This is the _ _ _ of my Blood'

To learn

Jesus my Lord I adore you.
Make me love you more and more.
O Sacrament most Holy,
O Sacrament Divine;
All praise and all thanksgiving be every moment thine.

To do

In the middle of this book you will find two sheets of thicker card. One half is covered with pictures of things you will see at Mass. On the back there is a word to tell you what it is.

You can make a domino game by colouring in the pictures and then cutting them all out carefully. Mix up the dominoes. Share them out equally with a friend or two. Decide who is going to start.

The first person puts down a domino and the next person puts down one with the same picture or word on, taking it in turns to do this until they are used up. If you have not got a matching one, you must miss your turn. The winner is the first one to use them all up. You can play with the dominoes either way up.

More to do

Make sure that you know how to make the sign of the cross and how to genuflect. Find out some things about your church: what is it called? How old is it? How many Masses are there each week? What other services can you go to?

?

QUESTION: What is the tabernacle?   ANSWER: The tabernacle is where the Eucharist is kept so that we can adore and pray before Jesus who is really present there.

QUESTION: What does the Real Presence mean?   ANSWER: The Real Presence means that Jesus is truly there in the host – the Blessed Sacrament.

18. Jesus comes to me in Communion

'The Body of Christ.'
'Amen.'

When we receive Holy Communion we are meeting Jesus himself. He comes to us to feed our souls and make us grow. He is really present in the host and the chalice under the outward forms of bread and wine.

Because the Eucharist is Jesus himself, we always go to Communion very humbly and with reverence. This means that we must be already thinking and praying about this wonderful moment. Listening to the prayers and readings of the Mass is the best way to do this.

Going up to receive Holy Communion, we have our hands joined in front of us and are quiet and full of love for Jesus. When our turn comes, the priest says to us 'The Body of Christ.' We answer 'Amen.' Then we make the **sign of the cross** and go quietly back to our places to make a silent prayer of thanks to God.

Your parents will tell you how they would like you to receive Communion. Some people stand and others kneel. Some receive the host straight on to their tongue and some receive in the hand. Some have just the host and others receive from the chalice as well. Whichever you do, do it with great care and respect. It is God's great gift to you.

God gives each of us great graces when we receive him in Communion. He makes us strong and healthy in our souls. Just as our bodies will weaken and die without food, so our souls need the Eucharist. It is our spiritual food for our journey to God. Holy Communion also gives us a glimpse of heaven. In the Bible, heaven is sometimes called a great feast. The Mass gives us an earthly taste of eternal life with God.

To write

Choose the right word to put into each one of the gaps:

Jesus himself is really .... in Holy

Communion. We must receive him with

.... The priest says to each

of us 'The Body of .... ' . We reply

' .... ' . We must thank God for his great

gift of the ....

The .... is the thin wafer of bread which

the priest consecrates. It becomes Jesus's Body. The wine

which becomes Jesus's Blood is taken from the ....

Eucharist   host   present   reverence

Amen   chalice   Christ

To learn

Prayers you can say quietly before, during and after Communion:

> Lord, I am not worthy that you should enter under my roof, but only say the word and my soul shall be healed.

> My Lord and My God!

> Jesus, true God and true Man, I adore you present in my soul.

> Lord Jesus, I thank you with all my heart for giving yourself to me in Holy Communion. What can I give you for all the graces you have given me?

More to do

Write your own short prayer, thanking God for giving himself to you in Holy Communion.

Make sure you know how to receive Communion – ask your parents how they would like you to do this.

Find out what you should wear for your First Holy Communion Mass.

? QUESTION: How should I get ready for receiving Communion?   ANSWER: We should prepare for Communion by being free from mortal sin and keeping the Eucharistic fast.
QUESTION: What is the Eucharistic fast?   ANSWER: Anyone who wants to receive Communion must not eat for one hour before.

What else have you learned? Test yourself

1. What miracle did Jesus do at Cana?
2. How many loaves and fishes did the boy bring to Jesus?
3. How many people did Jesus feed with the bread and fish?
4. What does 'Eucharist' mean?
5. What did God give the Israelite people to eat in the desert?
6. What is heaven?
7. What was the greatest feast of the year for the Jewish people?
8. What kind of bread was eaten at the Last Supper?
9. What words did Jesus say over the Last Supper bread?
10. Who sent Jesus off to be killed?
11. What did Simon of Cyrene do?
12. Where was Jesus put to death?
13. What do we call Jesus's rising from the dead?
14. What do we call the day when Jesus rose again?
15. What do we call the part of the Mass when the bread and wine become Jesus's Body and Blood?
16. What is the tabernacle?

Some more difficult ones – try them

17. What did Jesus mean when he said that he was like a Vine?
18. What did Jesus's death do for us?
19. What happens at the Consecration?
20. What is the Real Presence?

Turn the book round to see the answers on the opposite page.

Answers

1. He turned water into wine
2. Five loaves and two fishes
3. Five thousand people
4. 'Eucharist' means 'thanksgiving'
5. Manna
6. Heaven is living in happiness for ever with God
7. The Passover
8. Unleavened bread – without yeast
9. 'This is my Body which is given for you'
10. Pontius Pilate
11. Helped Jesus to carry his cross
12. On Calvary – a hill outside Jerusalem
13. The Resurrection
14. Easter Sunday
15. The Consecration
16. The Tabernacle is the place in the church where the Eucharist is kept

17. He meant that we are joined to him like branches and will wither and die if we cut ourselves off
18. Jesus's death redeemed us from sin and brought us back to God's friendship
19. At the Consecration God makes the bread and wine become the Body and Blood of Jesus
20. The Real Presence means that Jesus is truly there in the consecrated host and chalice

How many right answers did you get?

Glossary

Abraham   A great man of faith in the Old Testament, he obeyed God's call to go to the Promised Land.

Absolution   God's forgiveness given by the priest at the end of Confession.

Baptism   The first Sacrament: we are washed clean of Original Sin and begin our new life with God.

Bishops   The successors of the apostles who rule and guide the Church.

Blessed Sacrament   The Eucharist: Jesus's Body and Blood.

Chalice   The sacred vessel in which the wine is placed – the wine becomes the Blood of Jesus.

Church   The followers of Jesus who are baptised and believe in him, led by the Pope and Bishops.

Commandments   The ten laws which God gave to Moses on Mount Sinai so that the people could know God's will.

Communion   Receiving the sacrament of Jesus's Body and Blood.

Confession   The Sacrament in which we tell our sins and have them forgiven.

Conscience   The way in which God speaks to us in our hearts about what is right and wrong.

Consecration   The part of the Mass when the bread and wine become Jesus's Body and Blood.

Contrition   Sorrow for our sins – we say the Act of Contrition when we go to Confession.

Disciples   Jesus's followers.

Eucharist   The Sacrament of the Body and Blood of Jesus, with the outward sign of bread and wine.

Forgiveness   God accepts our sorrow for our sins and takes them away for us.

Genuflecting   Going down on one knee in front of the tabernacle to adore Jesus.

Good Friday   The day on which Jesus died for us on the cross on Calvary.

Grace   God's loving and saving help which he gives to us in the Sacraments.

Heaven   Living with God for ever in love and happiness.

Host   The small round wafer of unleavened bread which the priest consecrates in the Mass.

Incarnation   Jesus the Son of God became Man.

Jesus   The earthly name of the Son of God born as a Man – it means Saviour.

John   Jesus's cousin was John the Baptist; one of the first disciples was also called John.

Joseph   Jesus's foster father.

Mary   Jesus's mother: we also call her the Blessed Virgin, the Mother of God and Our Lady.

Mass   The Sacrament of the Eucharist and the Sacrifice on Calvary re-enacted.

Miracle   A wonderful event done by God which cannot be explained in any other way.

Mortal sins	Serious wrong doings which cut us off from God.
Moses	A great leader of Israel in the Old Testament who received the Ten Commandments from God.
Original sin	We are born with this sin which the first humans committed when they disobeyed God.
Passover	The great feast of the Jewish people when they remember their escape from Egypt.
Penance	Another word for Confession; it also means the act we do to make up for having sinned.
Pontius Pilate	The Roman leader who condemned Jesus to death.
Pope	The leader of the Catholic Church: he is the successor of St Peter.
Priests	Men who have been ordained and who say Mass and look after God's people.
Prophets	People in the Old Testament who spoke to Israel on God's behalf.
Real Presence	Jesus is truly there in the consecrated bread and wine.
Redeemed	Saved by Jesus's death: his sacrifice took our sins away.
Resurrection	Jesus's rising again from death on Easter Sunday morning.
Sacrifice	When we give up something to help others: Jesus gave up his life for us.
Sign of the cross	A simple prayer we make with actions to remind us of the cross, and of the three persons in one God.
Sin	A wrong doing which offends God and hurts other people.
Soul	The spiritual part of a human being which is made by God to be like him.
Tabernacle	The place in church where the Blessed Sacrament is kept.
Temple	The great place of worship for the Jewish people in Jerusalem in Jesus's time.
Twelve apostles	The men chosen by Jesus from his disciples to be his special followers.
Vestments	The clothes worn by the priest including the chasuble, the stole and the alb.
Worship	Humbling ourselves before God because he created us and we love and adore him.

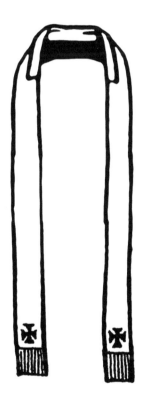